The Art of Marketing

By

Former Credit Union CEO

Nancy Gail Smith Mattox

Copyright 2017 © Nancy Gail Smith Mattox

ISBN 978-1-542-43216-0

Table of Contents

Nancy Gail Smith Mattox

Nancy Gail Smith Mattox

Chapter 1

It all began in the heart of America, God's country in the Appalachian Mountains, in Elizabethton, Tennessee, 15 miles from the Blue Ridgeway Parkway, where a tow headed little baby girl, Nancy Gail Smith, was born to Fred Elbert Smith and Phyllis Hampton Smith at the Franklin Clinic on April 30, 1953.

During this time of my life, little did I know that I was beginning my life's purpose of people helping people. Although neighbors were not close geographically, they were constantly trading products (garden vegetables, cows, pigs, etc.) so that the entire neighborhood did not lack for food and shelter.

After six weeks with my grandparents, Harvey Logan who was the city barber and antique collector and my grandmother , "Virgie" Virginia Johnson Hampton, my Father, Fred Smith took my mother, Phyllis and I and headed from Elizabethton, Tennessee to Jacksonville, Florida. My father moved his little family to Jacksonville, Florida to go to barbering school. After graduation, he went to work at a cigar factory called John H Swisher and Sons, producing King Edward Cigars. He became the supervisor over a very large and important department that filled the inside of cigars.

My mother also went to work at John H Swisher as a packer. She essentially ran an assembly line and packed the finished cigars into their packaging for the stores.

As both parents began their careers with the cigar factory, during orientation as new hires, they became members of King Edward Employees Credit Union. A not for profit cooperative that allowed payroll deductions for savings, Christmas clubs, and loan payments.

Thus began my love affair with Credit Unions, not for profit cooperatives with the mantra of "People Helping People." I always knew that when we needed money for emergencies and holidays such as Easter, Christmas, and Thanksgiving, the credit union would be available. It not only offered savings accounts and various types of loans, but also enabled customers to participate in Christmas clubs.

I was a very mature 5-year-old and visited the credit union on many occasions with my parents. Referring to the cashier as the "money lady," I would always tell her and my parents that I wanted to become a "money lady" someday and help others. I did not realize that I was indeed foretelling my future and subconsciously beginning my journey of helping others and becoming a part of the nonprofit credit union cooperation. The thought of people putting money in the credit union through payroll deduction for other people that needed money who would pay it back through payroll deduction really fascinated me. I became an instant "people helping people" person.

Summary:

As I grew up and began to understand the operations of Credit Unions, I realized that I would be able to learn more and use my people skills to continue to help people. My life's mission was determined by my ability to use compassion to people and helping them realizing their dreams using their finances.

*My mother, Phyllis Jean Young, Dolores Dubovsky Vice President
and my sister, Carolyn Aden at a Credit Union event*

Chapter 2

My journey down the road of helping people through the credit union began on June 1, 1969, at the age of 16 when I got my first job at the King Edward cigar factory and had to buy gas for the car to run the roads and visit. Employment at the cigar factory enabled me to become a member of the King Edward Employees Credit Union. I had money deducted from my paycheck that accumulated very quickly without me missing it or realizing it. When I got ready to buy my first car, you guessed it, King Edward Employees Credit Union, financed it and, I paid for it through payroll deduction.

I graduated from Andrew Jackson High School in Jacksonville, Florida on June 1, 1971 and married Rusty Mattox, a 1969 graduate, on February 26, 1972.

Summary:

Marketing the credit union is a captive audience was a charm. Credit Union employees had to go in the factory and help the employees with their finances. They were so passionate about their mission to help the employees reach their financial dreams.

Chapter 3

After graduating from High School and getting married, I started thinking of what I wanted to do, I began my career of "people helping people" and "promoting people reaching their dreams through finances" with Florida Telco Credit Union as a teller on March 1, 1972 and progressed upwards until I became a loan officer where I could really fulfil my destiny of helping people realize their dreams (cars, boats, homes, motorcycles, etc.). The position of a loan officer in credit unions is the most gratifying job in the World. You begin to really fine tune your skills as well as begin to use your core values to help people.

On January 1, 1973, I left Florida Telco Credit Union and went to work for the Jax Police Credit Union as the office manager. I trained under a wonderful credit union pioneer, Ms. Josephine Heard. Ms. Heard taught me everything about the internal operations of a credit union. One thing about Ms. Heard, she made me learn to use the 10-key adding machine. I had to practice on rows of numbers until I was at a speed that was acceptable to Ms. Heard. I will never forget my experiences and the teachings of Ms. Heard, a real task master. The credit union grew from $3 million to $15 million and added 3,000 new members during my tenure there.

On July 4th, 1977, I changed jobs again and went to St. Vincent's Hospital Federal Credit Union as the Manager. I also had a life-changing event and my second lifelong dream by giving birth to my only son on December 13, 1977. Having only one son gave me the time during my life to pursue my dream of people helping people in credit unions.

Summary:

I was so excited to be on my way. I now knew my mission in life. God had lead me to help people through cooperatives called Credit Unions. I gained the experience to market the credit union with passion. My compassionate spirit of helping people was really paying off. The gratification that I received was fantastic. I marketed the credit union by going to the potential members on the job to bring them to the credit union. This 4-year part of my journey propelled me to the crest. My passionate marketing of the credit union to the police officers barred none. We did promotions for the policemen like they had never experienced. We went to them on the job and made the credit union the most important benefit for their jobs. It worked and the credit union became a staple for the policeman.

This was the beginning!

Chapter 4

On August 1, 1979, my dream came true. I went to work for Seaboard Credit Union as a management trainee. The manager of the Credit Union, Ms. Jeannie Rasmussen, was the darling for the Seaboard Airline Railroad and had ran the credit union for 35 years, as she began to wind down toward retirement, she afforded me the opportunity to wind up and get ready for a 25 year ride as the manager/president of Seaboard Credit Union.

Ms. Rasmussen, another true credit union pioneer, was a task master also. She devoted nothing but service, service, and service to our members, the railroaders of Seaboard Airline Railroad. Ms. Rasmussen was a blond bombshell that literally everyone at Seaboard Airline Railroad knew because she worked for the railroad before taking on the credit union 35 years before.

Groundbreaking for new building with Jeanette Rasmussen

Nancy Gail Smith Mattox

I was blessed again to have another credit union pioneer to teach me the basics and core values of credit unions. This "people helping people" philosophy came up again and again in my life. I was then hooked for the next 25 years of my life. I was 25 years old when Ms. Rasmussen retired and left Seaboard Credit Union with me. My journey with Seaboard Credit Union and my lifelong dream of being in a position to help people came true!

As my lifelong dream and journey began on August 1, 1979, I pondered and wondered if I would really be able to help people throughout the next 25 years. I was so excited about my fantastic new position. I began as the bookkeeper and perfected this job within the year. Learning the workflow of the money coming in (through members' payroll deductions) and money going out (by way of loans that were paid back through members' payroll deductions), I was in awe of how assets continued to grow. People were so in need of financial guidance and help!

Seaboard Credit Union was $15 million in assets and had 3100 members when I began in 1979. It was an awesome and overwhelming task, knowing that I had to manage that much money and help that many people to obtain financial happiness. My mentors Ms. Heard, from Jax Police Credit Union, and Ms. Jeannie Rasmussen, from Seaboard Credit Union, were always with me in spirit. Their words and teachings helped me overcome the fear, and I began to tackle the tasks involved with my dreams.

My mantra at Seaboard Credit Union was that I was in the business of helping people reach their dreams, whether it be saving for their wedding, their first home, their first child, their children's college, their cars, their boats, their homes, and the evolvement of their dreams!

The Credit Union Movement's mantra was, "people helping people"! Between my mantra and the movement's mantra, Seaboard Credit Union had it covered! Here we go! Forward with the adventure of my life and my lifelong dream!

Summary:

Never quit dreaming. Always continue to believe and chase your dreams. If you are dedicated and purpose driven, your dreams will evolve. My positive attitude of people helping people was the catalyst for my success and the success of Seaboard Credit Union. Guerrilla marketing made it happen. In your face relentless marketing made it happen.

Chapter 5

It is time to go back to the beginning and explain the Credit Union Movement a movement of credit union cooperatives with the mantra of "people helping people."

Seaboard Credit Union was chartered in November 1926 by seven Seaboard Airline Railroad Employees pooling $156. Seven railroad workers began this wonderful not for profit cooperative, called Seaboard Credit Union. Let the fun begin.

Seaboard had only three secretaries, treasurers of the board of directors and managers from 1926 until 2004. I was the third in the history of the credit union and had a 25- year run. The best part of my life was spent helping members of the credit union. I always considered the credit union made dreams come true! Anything you dreamed of you could have with the help of the Credit Union.

In a word, I was 25 with an opportunity to live my lifelong dream of helping people. I was so excited with my new career. Young, passionate, and compassionate were my qualities! My passion of loving the members and credit union NEVER waned!

Summary:

Failure was not an option for me and Seaboard Credit Union. Marketing was the key. An "AHA" formula: Attitude – Humor – Action. Success breeds success. Always keep your compassion for helping your clients.

Chapter 6

My tenure with Seaboard Credit Union began on August 1, 1979. The month that I began the credit union, we had $15 million in assets and 3,200 members. All the members from the Seaboard Airline Railroad later merged with another railroad in the Northeast, called Chessie Railroad System. After the merger in 1985, the name of our sponsor became CSX Corporation and had a whole bunch of employees, who became potential members for Seaboard.

Seaboard Railroad and Chessie Railroad merged to create the CSX Railroad.

There were 56 credit unions, up and down the Eastern Seaboard of the United States, which is the territory that CSX, our sponsor serviced. CSX had 62,000 employees at that time, so there were plenty of potential members for all 56 credit unions. The railroad credit unions collaborated once a year. We discussed furloughs, closing of railroad shops, and payroll deductions that we received. In 1990, CSX stopped issuing payroll checks to the employees and mandated direct deposit for all employees. This was a blessing for the credit unions. We actually would get our money from our members electronically. At the same time, CSX started charging the credit unions 25 cent for each payroll deduction that each credit union received. This was a very large expense for the credit unions, but oh so important, for us to continue to receive the payroll deductions. The payroll deductions paid the employee/members loan payments, funded their savings and checking accounts. Win-Win for all!

From 1979, the time I began working there, to 1991, Seaboard Credit Union remained a pure railroad credit union because it allowed only employees and their immediate family members to join.

In December 1979 (2 weeks after I started working there), we celebrated the grand opening of a new credit union building 2500 square feet of pure beauty. The credit union had a drive thru for convenience and four 4 real teller stations. The credit union was right across the street from the CSX railroad yard, with about 1000 railroaders. What a coup for Seaboard Credit Union. We were like a high speed train without any brakes! Nothing could stop us now! And wow, I was the new President that was going to lead the credit union for the next 25 years. What a blessing for me and the credit union!

The grand opening of the new building was the most awesome party that I had ever been to in my life. There were so many important dignitaries and special people.

Nice new building, the CSX Corporation across the street, then we were ready to rock and roll. There was a large amount of marketing and growing to do during my first year at Seaboard Credit Union.

Inside of new credit union Building.

Chapter 7

We wrote our first marketing plan and started marketing on a regular basis through a quarterly newsletter. During the planning session of the board of directors, we really decided to advertise the $2,000 in the Life Savings Program for our members. This program really attracted deposits, which we could use to loan to our existing members and our potential new members.

Many credit unions offered The Life Savings Program since their inception. The Life Savings Program was a 100% matching program for up to $2000 to every member (depositor) that had at least $2000 in their savings account. These accounts were the low earning accounts and the cost of the program was not very much. The Credit Union insurance company, Cuna Mutual Insurance Society, actually backed the program with the premiums that Seaboard Credit Union paid. At the members' death, their beneficiaries were given the savings, the dividends on the account balance and an extra $2000 for the Life Savings Program.

Our marketing plan showed that we would advertise this program, bring in new deposits and loan the money to our members. Potential members must be made aware of this program. Seaboard Credit Union increased their LS program to $2000 from $1000 in 1979, which was not the case for other credit unions. This move gave us a competitive edge. This is every inexpensive program actually drew more deposits and new members to Seaboard. It was the beginning of the phenomenal growth that would take place over the next 25 years.

We had bulletproof glass installed over our teller stations. We had to explain to members that we were not trying to lock them out, but with our growth, we had to keep our staff safe. The neighborhood was beginning to deteriorate. CSX and Seaboard Credit Union implemented many safety rules for our staff, customers and members. One of our Board members was on the security force for CSX Corporation, and he tested the bulletproof glass with a 357 magnum pistol. The glass did not shatter, but absorbed the bullet.

State of the art bullet proof glass in lobby to protect tellers

Quarterly newsletters were a real hit with members. We had contests built into the bodies of our newsletter articles so that we could determine who was reading the newsletters. We would hide several account numbers in the newsletters and when the members found it and called us, received $100 in their account. We also advertised the special rates on savings and loans. If we had any promotions going on, we would use the newsletters to broadcast to our members. We inserted the newsletters into the statement mail outs, monthly.

By the beginning of 1979, we had 3100 members with $15 million in assets. At the end of the year, we had 3,400 members with $16.5 million in assets.

Summary:

We were now in a position and had the professional bank building with safe deposit boxes to turn up the guerrilla marketing. At this point, we started reaching out to our potential clients. We went to them. We catered to them. The growth was outstanding because of the marketing.

Chapter 8

As we began another year, there was a lot of planning of exciting events to promote growth and profits. Regulators were happy with our progress and, we received a code 1, which was considered the best, from them.

Our marketing plan for 1980 was to increase membership and to increase the number of savings and loans. We had very aggressive growth goals of 10% for 1980.

In April 1980, I decided that we needed to give some recognition to our staff. We needed to let our hair down and have some fun. We had our very first Staff Easter Egg Hunt! The hidden eggs were filled with money, gift cards, and restaurant certificates. The eggs were hidden all over the credit union. We had the hunt after our weekly staff meeting at 7:30 a.m. Staff had a fantastic time, appreciated the recognition, and wanted to do more work to grow the credit union.

Every year, during the month of January, we had our regulatory Annual Meeting of members. The Annual Meeting included lots of prizes and food for those who attended. This event was the event of the year for our members. They dressed up and came to hear about the condition of the credit union. Because it was member oriented, we held four different annual meetings every Saturday in January. We traveled in the State of Florida where we had a predominance of members. We held the meetings at our beautiful main office in Jacksonville, Florida, and then in Leesburg, Tallahassee, and Miami,
Florida.

These annual meetings were well attended. We always presented the past year successes and what we had planned for the next year. The board of directors and all staff had to attend the Jacksonville meeting. The board of directors and the management team had to attend the other three meetings.

During the annual meetings, we had as many as 1000 members in attendance. We would set up specialty booths in our lobby (with staff manning them) to display our best products and services.

During 1980, we also began to order extra newsletters to be hand delivered to the CSX buildings. We would take the newsletters to the desks of the employees, member or not.
We used this exercise to solicit new members.

On June 15, 1980, we participated in our first Juvenile Diabetes Walk, which was sponsored by CSX. We had a contest for the logo that would be on our tee shirts. Members and Staff helped created the Seaboard logo that we placed on our shirts each year. The winner of the logo that we chose received $50. We participated in this walk for many years in the future. Our first team consisted of staff members and their families, along with members. We had 50 people on our first team. Seaboard Credit Union raised over $2,500 for juvenile diabetes from the fundraiser walk.

We reached all our goals for 1980. We now have 3700 members and $17.8 million in assets

In 1981, we had so much fun and many exciting things happen. We planned our first data processing conversion with a new computer. We were finally leaving the early 1970's ledger card system and moving to automation. We prepared a very special computer room with separate air conditioning and lots of fireproofing. The heart of the credit union would be in this room.

The computer conversion took 6 six months to implement. We were so excited. We would have more time to market to new potential members. We would be able to continue on our venture of growing the credit union with quality members, quality loans, and assets. We were so proud of our progress and the new data processing system. We actually could have time away from the ledger cards to market, market.

We became bolder with our marketing efforts. When we delivered newsletters to the CSX employees' desks, we were now well liked enough that we could talk to the employees and help them make their financial dreams come true!

During that year, we decided to begin to market with a promotion to bring in a family member or coworker and get $5. We began to utilize the clause in our charter that members were allowed to sponsor their family members into the credit union. In doing so, they would receive $5 for each member that they brought into the credit union. We experienced phenomenal growth with the promotion.

We also paid existing members $5 to bring their coworkers into the credit union. As new members signed up that gave us more and more potential members to join the credit union, which was a perpetual number of potential members and growth!

We were continuing on the road to success. My dreams for the credit union were really coming true.

As our marketing efforts were beginning to pay off, I wondered how I could keep the enthusiasm going with our staff. Staff needed to believe that Seaboard was the only financial institution for CSX employees and their families. I had to keep them motivated. Seaboard Board of Directors were good at approving many functions to keep staff interested. I actually could say at that point that our staff was so motivated that they lived for Seaboard Credit Union. Without this enthusiasm, I am sure that Seaboard would not have prospered and helped so many members reach their hopes and dreams!

Marketing promotion in the lobby of the international Company, CSX Corporation.

We began to have employee appreciation functions every six months. Staff would be so excited about these functions that I believe they stayed with the credit union longer than most employees at other financial institutions.

Seaboard Board of Directors always approved budget dollars for our employee functions. I always tried to plan fun events that would bring us closer together. I always believed that I could get more work out of the employees if I recognized them for their great works.

We began to have our holiday party (which included our spouses) on a paddle boat that went up and down the St. John's River. During these parties, we could see the magnificent city of Jacksonville at night, including the CSX building, where so many of our potential members worked. We would have staff decide the menu and many, many times we would let our families prepare the food.

With the end of another year, I was so excited. Our membership had increased to 4000 members with $20 million in assets. Wow, we surpassed two milestones: over 4000 members and over $20 million in assets. So much success for my first two years at the helm of Seaboard Credit Union!

Summary:

Along with the guerrilla marketing, we implemented promotions and staff enthusiasm into our marketing plan. The plan was working. The marketing was working. We were growing and growing.

Chapter 9

Going into 1982, my third year as President, we began with adding to our marketing plan to continue our success of growing our credit union. We knew if we continued to get new members, all the other products and services would grow too. We still just had savings, certificates, and consumer loans (no mortgage loans). Our motto became, "We offer services and products to complete your DREAMS!" We were still sticking to our roots of, "People helping People."

We added more CSX buildings to our marketing plan. We began to deliver our newsletters to any place where CSX employees were. If they had community events, safety meetings, three shifts of employees at 24-hour building, and any function of CSX, we became synonymous with the company.

We had representatives at every function that we heard about and the board of directors, which worked for CSX, got us invited to invitation-only functions. We participated fully with all of these functions. We had tables set up with our newsletters and brochures of our products and services, we had rate boards with our savings and loans rates, we donated door prizes, we donated time, we donated money, and anything else that would bring attention to Seaboard. We meant to be THE credit union for CSX Corporation. Remember there were 50 other credit unions up and down the eastern seaboard that also serviced the employees of CSX.

And that we did! Vice Presidents of the railroad that were banking with us gave us a lot of latitude with the employees of CSX. The VPs knew that we would give them plenty of recognition and credit for our success, and we also donated time, people, and money for their projects.

By the end of 1982, our assets were $22 million and we had 4,500 members. Wow! Really growing and reaching our goals.

Summary:

Competition was really heating up. The credit union's name was becoming known because of the marketing and great service. We were an institution to be reckoned with. In your face marketing, going to potential worksites where our clients were, promotions, and staff enthusiasm was the key to success. My passion was real!

Chapter 10

The years 1983 and 1984 brought many, many successes to Seaboard Credit Union. We began to have annual planning sessions with the management team and the board of directors. These sessions gave us a roadmap of where we were going and how to get there. We came to consensus that we would continue our very successful marketing plan, which included what we call "guerilla marketing." This concept was an advertising strategy in which low-cost (we didn't much money) unconventional means (newsletters on every desk at CSX) was utilized in a localized network to promote our products and services.

Planning sessions with the Board of Directors were key to our plan of success.

Good ole roll up your sleeves and plan for the future.

We created our children and youth club accounts. Our younger children's club (newborn – 12 years) was extremely popular. Parents and grandparents gave monetary gifts to their children and grandchildren and placed the money in their club accounts. The name of this club account was the Dalmation Club. We had white passbooks with black spots (like a Dalmatian), and we created pink and blue passbooks for the newborns.

In October 1983, we had "trick or treat" at the credit union for the Dalmation Club. We actually set up the lobby, carnival style with booths that staff ran with different games (go fish, apple bobbing, rubber ducky race, putt-putt golf, and fortune telling. Each booth allowed winners (everyone was a winner), prizes were given out, trick or treating at each booth, and pictures of the children in their costumes. Parents loved this safe environment for their children. We even had a costume contest with several categories. Winners received $50 in their accounts.

The name of our youth club accounts was the X-Generation. We had special seminars and functions at the credit union for the teenagers who regularly attended. We included contests and training on finances for them.

We also had the Staff Recognition on the paddle boat again that year. This time we had it professionally catered, so our staff's family would not have to work so hard. All staff members and board members attended. That attendance made my heart sing. Coworkers wanted to actually spend time with each other after work. This was a very cohesive group of employees and team.

Fun with Staff

Executive team at Seaboard Credit Union

More fun with staff!

Nancy Gail Smith Mattox

By now, we were 4,700 members strong, very well capitalized, had $23 million in assets and very strong as a credit union. Regulators were still giving us a code 1, the best! A huge milestone passed, more than 4,700 members.....

Summary:

We learned a valuable lesson during this time. We understood that happy staff makes for a happy credit union. We needed all staff to be motivated to pull off the aggressive growth goals of the credit union. Guerilla marketing takes energy, passion and enthusiasm.

Chapter 11

Beginning in 1984, we stopped having annual meetings at four different cities. We had too many members who were not in those cities, the railroad was closing those offices and we simply needed to include all 3000 members in our annual meeting process. The actual meeting was help at our main office. We still promoted the annual meeting, but we cut out the cash door prizes and started to cut down on the refreshments. Instead of a full meal, we had light refreshments. We did not want our out of town members who could not attend to be left out. We used the money that was previously spent on the four annual meetings, we spent on promotions in which members were given cash rewards for bringing in new members and for the services that they participated in.

The planning session this year was totally devoted to how we were to continue to grow and maintain our great member services and profitability. We included in our plan to begin to double the square footage of our existing building. We started evaluating the costs and effort needed to expand our building from 2500 square feet to 5000 square feet with more capabilities to give our members better and quicker service. Hint: more drive ups, an ATM on the building, and safe deposit boxes…..

Our annual meeting that year was a real hit! So many members attended, so much fun, so many refreshments. We started to let the members know about the plans for the credit union to expand, but continued to focus primarily on the railroad.

Before we could even plan for this, we decided to give our previous secretary/treasurer and third manager of the credit union recognition for making her plans reality for Seaboard Credit Union. She was responsible of the 2500 square feet that we were housed in that allowed us to grow to $23 million and 2,700 members.

We dedicated the building to this woman in May 1984 and had a reception in her honor. The turnout for this dedication was fantastic. We had a fantastic time and our older members who remembered "Ms. Jenny" also enjoyed the visit and loved our credit union even more!

Dedication of Building in honor of Ms. Jeannette Rasmussen

Seaboard Credit Union was progressing. The most exciting project that we had ever had was placing an ATM in the CSX corporation headquarters building lobby in September 1984. Because we had converted to an exemplary data processing system a few years back (great planning), we were able to drop our first ATM when the time was right. This project gave us many opportunities to advertise our "high touch, high tech" plan as well as being where CSX railroaders met.

We had a huge promotion to celebrate our first ATM. We were able to have a real presence at the CSX headquarters which had employees in the building working 24 hours per day. The ATM was located in the open lobby of the building that allowed visitors to come in and utilize it. This meant more transactions, meant more revenue for Seaboard. We made money off that ATM, we got more members because of the ATM, and we received priceless exposure for Seaboard Credit Union with CSX.

By the end of 1984, our plans were in place for the renovation and addition to our main office. How appropriate for our vision to expand so tremendously during the year 1984 ... Our assets went $25 million (wow!) and our membership was a whopping 5100. Look at the big picture. We were well on our way and far surpassing my dreams.

The year 1985 proved to be a very exciting year! The growth of Seaboard Credit Union just blew everyone's mind. We had accomplished so much in such a few six short years.

In January, we began the 2500 square feet addition and renovation of the existing 2500 square feet, an updated look for an updated progressive credit union. By March 1985, we were moving into the new space.

Our new space had all the products and services that any financial institution had. We have four, drive through windows, an ATM on the building, a children's play area and safe deposit boxes.... We were state of the art.

We were able to really implement the guerilla marketing plan because we had enough office space to accommodate the massive growth that was in store. We continued with our visits to the outlying buildings that had our potential members working there.

We helped federal regulators by merging a smaller credit union that was in financial trouble. We were able to begin to growing our credit union with mergers and acquisitions.

The first credit union that we merged had 1300 members and $3 million in assets. Their members and our members were supercharged to have a great credit union as part of their benefit package. The credit union's mantra of people helping people was alive and well. We were in the market place to sell DREAMS! Anything our members could dream of, we would help them achieve.

Seaboard Credit Union had discovered another way to have quality growth with acquisitions and mergers. And now we had the building with all the amenities to be a real financial institution to our members. Growth was awesome!

The open house for our addition and renovation was very well attended by the Westside of Jacksonville Chamber of Commerce and businesses. City dignitaries were so excited about a business spending money in the neighborhood. CSX was beginning to plan to spend millions of dollars on a state of the art dispatching center.

By the end of 1985, we were 5800 members strong and had assets of $27.7 million.

Summary:

What can I say! A textbook case study of guerilla marketing and promotion at its best. Hard work and working your plans will work. Set your plan and goals and go for them. Passion and hard work will make it happen.

Chapter 12

Since 1985 brought us the state of art facility that we needed to grow the credit union, in 1986 we began to research an update to our data processing system. We began with USERS Incorporated as our data processing system in 1981 and now were the time to upgrade the system. We were the first credit union in the United States to purchase the MS4000. There was a huge presentation at the USERS meeting in June 1986. We had the system fully upgraded and was using it by December 1986.

New safe deposit boxes were a draw to members, existing and new. We began to use another measuring tool, services per member. We were trying to maximize the use of our products and services. We placed more emphasis on selling our products and services to existing members. Most promotions were to make sure that members were using our products and services. We considered, checking accounts, direct deposit, each type of loan, safe deposit boxes, ATM cards, Christmas clubs, and savings accounts.

The annual planning session with the staff and board of directors was very special this year. We had to complete a five-year growth plan and marketing plan. We had to set our goals for growth. We had a lot of growing to do!

We really needed to reward our staff for the hard work this year. The Christmas party was fantastic. We had a computer conversion, added many new products and services, grew the credit union to $30.6 million in assets and 6200 members. We far surpassed our goals set by the board of directors as well as my internal goals for the credit union.

The Christmas party in 1986 was a blast. We had it at the Yacht Club with a Gambling theme. We had roulette wheels and black jack tables. The staff enjoyed dressing up, letting their hair down, and networking with their coworkers. This type of networking made the staff realize that we appreciated their hard work, and that we supported them 100%. It also showed that we expected just as much enthusiasm the following year! One of the secrets of our success was a happy staff and these functions created that!

Wow! Oh! Wow. We are on a roll and on target. People helping People, our motto.....And making dreams come true for our members. We were in the groove, we were growing our membership, our loan portfolio, our asset base, and helping so many members and potential members. I had been working at the credit union seven years, as the CEO and could not have been happier (time flies when you are having fun!). We still had our destiny to fulfill.

Summary:

We emcompassed the mantra of "High Touch – High Tech" We had to upgrade our technology to make the high touch marketing work. We were able to perform our in house duties on the road where ever we were doing our face to face marketing.

Chapter 13

In 1987, we continued to go to our potential members. We were invited to many safety meetings of our SEGS (select employee groups that were allowing us to serve their employees with all their financial needs). Getting into the safety meetings was a coup! We were able to bring the breakfast, serve the breakfast, and serve them all the financial services that they needed. We began to be known with our groups, as the credit union that would come to them and make their staff meetings and orientation meetings better with food, giveaways, and financial service beyond belief!

One special meeting was the railroad employee appreciation meeting in Waycross, Georgia, in September, which was the hottest time of the year in the South. We rented a huge rolling barbeque pit and supplied the full meal for over a 1000 employees, members and potential members. This function opened a lot of doors for us with our groups. We opened 52 accounts at this function, which more than compensated us for working in the heat at our potential members worksites. I think we found another niche' for Seaboard Credit Union.

After this function, we began to schedule more functions, anywhere that our potential members were meeting.

Funny story of how we got in with the railroad. One of our vice presidents finally got a meeting with the Executive Vice President of the railroad. I was so proud of her. She went to the meeting with the proposal for Seaboard Credit Union to be the financial institution of choice for the employees of the railroad. You must understand that both the Seaboard Airline Railroad and the Chessie Railroad Systems had more than 75 credit unions up and down the eastern sea board, so this was a very bold proposal. After sitting down at the EVP's desk, his assistant offered coffee, our VP accepted the coffee offer. She was so nervous that she accidently spilt her coffer all over his desk. She promised that she would make it up to him and clean it up. Actually this broke the ice, as she left his office and the meeting, he actually joined our credit union, moved all financial services to us, endorsed us, and gave us access to hundreds of meeting of the railroad.

Hold your horses, we were ready to go! This year we really amped up the guerilla marketing. We went where our members/potential members were. We were out of town marketing, we were in the buildings of our SEGS marketing, and we were becoming known as the credit union to do business with, even though we were not in the same town as the members. We also created another new mantra, "High tech/High touch!" We were able to fulfill this mantra with our new data processing system and our becoming road warriors. We meant to go where our members were, and we meant to serve our members through technology!

By the end of 1987, we had 6,700 members and $33.5 in assets. We had another fantastic year. Our members were happy as we knew because 99% said in a full membership survey, that they were very satisfied with our service. This made my heart beat faster. I was so happy.

In 1988 and 1989, we really used the goodwill of our SEGS. We had doors opened to all kind of functions (staff meetings, new employee orientations, safety meetings, employee appreciations, and association meetings).

Summary:

Know your customers. Know your targets for marketing. Study your competition. Always, always get up earlier and be ready before the competition. We used every tool possible to work our marketing plan.

Chapter 14

By the end of 1988, we had opened our second branch in Jacksonville, Florida, on the South side of town in an area called Southpoint. Our members across the river were very happy to have an office to go to. This branch grew very rapidly and helped us reach our very aggressive goals for membership, assets, and loans. We also had aggressive goals for a return on assets in order to continue to build our capital. We could not afford to let the growth go unbalanced. Regulators were very happy that we had a balanced growth plan, which included a net worth (capital to credit unions) goal.

In July, we had the biggest promotion that we had ever had at our credit union. It was an outside function on the gazebo on the lake at our Southpoint branch. It was extremely hot (97 degrees), but the heat did not deter us. The promotion was called Old Fashion Days at Seaboard. We were offering 25 cents hot dogs, sodas, and chips. We actually purchased 3000 hot dogs with all the fixings. We had a hot dog wagon on site, cooked and we served the hot dogs, sodas, and chips.
We served more than 2500 members at this member appreciation promotion. Once again, we exceeded our members' expectations. It was a daylong event we allowed all staff members to come and help, and we received a lot of free press for this promotion. I was labeled at Boss's Day that year as the "Weiner Queen" and was given a trophy.

Gazebo at our Southpoint branch. The biggest promotion that we ever had. Huge Success.

3,000 hot dogs and cold drinks served to over 3000 potential members and members

As I have stated before, the CSX Corporation, our primary sponsor with 35,000 employees, decided to invest millions of dollars right across the street from our Westside (original) office. In March

1989, we were invited to the 21st century and the dedication of the Kenneth C. Dufford Transportation Center at 3019 Warrington Street, Jacksonville, Florida. Our credit union's address was 3020 Warrington Street. This center was a $4 million renovation that created a state of the art transportation center. The inside of the center actually was very dark and had a circular interior with the CSX railroad tracks electronically displayed with red and yellow lights that portrayed where every train was located on the system, from Miami, Florida to Baltimore, Maryland. It was a Star Wars building for the railroad.

Talk about new life and recognition, there were many, many dignitaries from all over the world at this dedication and so was Seaboard Credit Union. We actually got to rub shoulders with the management of CSX Corporation as well as World leaders, all experiencing the 21st Century. This center had over 2,500 employees, and we had access to all of them for membership in our credit union.

We were so excited and so thankful for the board of directors that guided us to this awesome growth and allowed us to be very aggressive. After all, they worked with other executives of the railroad, had to face them and stand up for our actions, and still agreed to allow us to continue to grow. As recognition, we had professional portraits taken of the nine board members and posted them in our Board Room.

The planning session was great this year. Our board of directors were always acutely in tune with us, they always attended, and participated in the planning session. As a result, we always had a roadmap of where we were going and tactics to get there. I was so appreciative of our board members and the active role that they took in the success of Seaboard Credit Union.

The employee recognition and Christmas party this year had a fantastic theme that the staff chose. It was a luau. Everyone was recognized for their hard work and their part in our success. These events always made the staff want to work harder for the credit union and our members.

By the end of 1989, we had reached an unbelievable membership growth goal to 8,000 members.and an asset goal of $40.5 million. I truly felt like I was dreaming the sweetest dream ever. We were serving our members so well, we were creating the kind of products and services, and we were growing by leaps and bounds. The credit union and I loved to help people, and we were helping over 8000 members. Wow!

The next year two years (1990 and 1991) proved even more exciting than the past 10 years of my tenure and the credit union's exciting growth and stability!

At this point, we felt we should separate the employee recognition from the Christmas party. In June, (hot, hot, hot), we had an incredible Employee recognition event. We had 100% participation of both board of directors and staff. Again, we were firm believers that in order to serve our members and grow our credit union, we had to have happy employees. This type of event helped keep our employees happy!

This year we began an annual event of judging the Halloween Costume contest at the Southpoint CSX building (over 3000 employees of CSX). We needed to keep access to this building to continue our guerilla marketing, so we gladly accepted.

We provided lunch for the members/potential members and judged their costume contest. We gleaned a great amount of free publicity in the CSX employee newsletter and the Jacksonville press. It was always a huge event. We always served more than 2000 hotdogs, sodas, and chips. It was always a great time for the members, potential members, and staff.

The planning session this year continued to build on our plans of going to our potential members. Because the railroad was planning to move 10,000 employees to Baltimore, Maryland from Jacksonville, Florida, and 3500 of those were our members, we planned on opening our 3rd branch in Baltimore, Maryland.

Summary:

Big things happening. A huge milestone of $40 million in assets. Promotions all over the country. Signing up members everywhere. Marketing, marketing, marketing.

Chapter 15

In March 1991, we opened our Baltimore Branch in downtown Baltimore, transferred a fantastic VP that had been with us for many years to Baltimore to manage it, and had a great grand opening. The branch was a state of art building with an ATM on the building. Our 3500 members who were transferred to Baltimore were so excited that their credit union was going with them, and they loved the branch manager. This branch brought continued new members, new loans, and new checking accounts to us, and allowed us to reach our aggressive growth goals.

New branch in downtown Baltimore Maryland.

We had another fun promotion in September 1991 in order to continue our guerilla marketing. We began the "we are sweet and on fire for you" membership promotion. We made 5,000 packets with clear cellophane, tied with white ribbons that contained a chocolate Hershey's kiss and a fireball. We delivered these to the desks of 5,000 members/potential members before 7:00 a.m., which was to 24 floors of the CSX building downtown. Once again, Seaboard Credit Union was the buzz word in that huge building downtown. Remember that we had already placed an ATM in that building in 1984 and now we were showing them that we are still here and growing strong. We gleaned many new membership opportunities because of this promotion.

We continued to surpass our growth goals on membership, assets, loans, and net worth. We had reached another milestone. I couldn't have been happier! We were a very large and successful credit union in Jacksonville, Florida. We were talked about in our credit union community. Our assets had reached $50 million and we had over 9,200 members. We were well on our way to making our mark in the credit union community of the country.

As we began my 13th year (1992) as CEO/President of Seaboard Credit Union, we had experienced very much success. Being a $50 million credit union put us into a new and very competitive market. We had to address this new credit union world for us. We renewed our five years growth and marketing plans. We knew that if we kept doing what we were doing, we would continue to succeed. For the next few years, we kept a steady pace of growth by helping our existing members to increase their product and service use with us, by going to places where our potential members met, and by upgrading our phone system.

With the upgrade of our phone system, we created a new department called the Call Center. We discovered that we had to have a better accounting of the phone calls from our members and the level of service that we were giving. After all, we were advertising, "high touch/high tech" in every advertising piece. Since we were continuing the guerilla marketing and going to our potential members with promotion, we needed to make sure that we were taking care of business after the promotions when people started calling in.

The new phone system had a call accounting system. This system kept track of all calls, the duration of the calls, hang ups, drops, and even recorded the member service representative service calls. We were able to monitor our calls through technology and make sure that we were putting our money where our mouths were. We discovered that we were right on target with the call center. The representatives were the best of the best, thus providing the best of the best service to our new members calling in from all over the southeast United States.

During all this technology, I still refused to allow an automated attendant to answer our main phone lines and route the calls. At this upgrade, we still had a person, sometimes two people, answering all phone calls and routing to the proper department. The call answering script went like this, "We are having a great day at Seaboard Credit Union, thank you for calling and how may I direct your call?" This script was tested and tested and worked extremely well. Our telephone receptionists had to have special talents. After all, our telephones were the window to the heart of our credit union.

Our annual meeting this year was held at the home office building on the Westside of Jacksonville, on Warrington Street. We had a great number of members who attended. Refreshments and great information on our financial health was presented to those in attendance.

Funny from a member at the annual meeting. A previous chair of the board's widow came up to me and said that she was so excited to come to the annual meetings so that she could see what kind of hairdo that I had each year. As I looked back at the 14 years of pictures at the annual meetings, sure enough, I had a different hair style at each meeting. This warmed my heart. This conversation reminded yet again of why I joined the credit union movement to help people. I actually made a difference in thousands of peoples' lives, and this was a fantastic example.

Huge numbers of members at our Annual Meetings every year.
They were so excited about their Credit Union

We had an annual member picnic that year! Something a little different for us. We invited our members, and focused on our child account, the "Dalmation Club." We cooked hot dogs and hamburgers, we rented a huge grill to bring to the park. We had hayrides for the children in attendance. Our members had a great time. And once again, we were able to show them that we really appreciated them.

In the fall, we had a huge promotion at the CSX building in downtown and Southpoint. Thousands of members stopped by our booth, received giveaways, visited with staff, joined their family members, and received $5 for each new member that they brought in. We had to stay in constant contact with our SEGs. We also had a promotion at a paper company SEG. We cooked lunch for more than 500 employees. We judged the Costume Contest at Southpoint again this year. These promotions were the bane of our existence. They propelled our credit union into tremendous growth. We had finally become a household name to our members, and we were their financial institution of choice. Our products and services to each member ratio were above average with the national averages for credit union. All our hard work was paying off.

The Christmas party this year was very special. We held it at a local country club with a live band. It was a very dressy affair. Staff and board of directors enjoyed dressing up for the holidays, getting their pictures made, and really having a good time in an elegant atmosphere. Lots of fantastic camaraderie and fun!

Summary:

This chapter is very special to me. We had many great happenings for marketing this year. We continued with our guerrilla marketing by taking our dog and pony show to every area where our clients met. Another secret to marketing, go where your clients are every chance you get.

Nancy Gail Smith Mattox

Chapter 16

As we continued on to 1993 and 1994, we were continuing with our five-year plan. We were far surpassing all financial goals, membership goals, and asset growth goals while keeping pace with our net worth growth goal. We continued to receive the highest ratings from our state and federal regulators.

The road warriors were in full force. In an effort to reach potential members, we had many out of town promotions we spent a lot of time on the road going to SEG locations within the State of Florida, as well as Maryland, Kentucky, Tennessee, North, South Carolina, and Georgia.

We completed two more mergers with a credit union in Atlanta, Georgia, and a credit union in Jacksonville, Florida, both were prompted by the federal regulators. Because we had many members and potential members in those areas, we were more than happy to absorb the credit unions. We experienced phenomenal growth with these mergers. Many potential growth opportunities came with these mergers.

We had a special promotion in December 1993 at our Westside office. We had Santa there and took pictures of the children (young and old) with Santa. Another huge success! Everyone that came to the member appreciation received a gift (giveaway). We signed up more children and grandchildren as members.

In October 1993, we were instrumental in getting the Chairman of the National Credit Union Administration, Norman DaMours to attend a meeting on International Credit Union Day in Jacksonville, Florida. We were honored for Mr. DaMours to come to Seaboard Credit Union for a visit. He wanted to visit one of the most progressive and successful credit unions in the Country. This was an awesome honor for Seaboard Credit Union

Our employee appreciation in 1994 was called "Wow, what superstars!" We continued to believe that happy employees made happy members, which allowed us the great success and growth of Seaboard Credit Union. All staff and board of directors attended and had a fantastic time! Another successful employee function!

By the end of 1994, we were very well capitalized and were a very large credit union with assets were over $65 million and over 12,300 happy, happy members. My heart continued to sing! I was living my dream job and had more success that could ever have been imagined! Mine and Seaboard's blessings to our members were truly being returned to us 1000 fold.

As 1995, rapidly approached, we had to update our five-year plan. The new plan included a plan to purchase land in Southpoint (the growing business community) and build a new signature home office building. My excitement continued to grow. More work meant nothing to me and the credit union. We had had such success over the past 15 years and now it was time to move on and up!

The annual meeting in January 1995, was held at the Westside home office. The excitement was high as we told of our plans to build a new main office. Of course, we would not abandon or forget our roots on the Westside of Jacksonville. The office would remain a very large branch of Seaboard Credit Union. Members and staff enjoyed the refreshments and the networking at the annual meeting.

In the fall of 1995, we accepted the invitation to attend a very large promotion and trade show, "Jax Port Fest," where we expected 5,000 people to visit our booth. This was more of a community festival to celebrate the Jacksonville Port. We spent weeks preparing for our booth at this trade show. We had five staff members to man the booth. We gave out candy and had a door prize drawing for all who filled out the slip with name, phone number, address, and email address. The door prize drawing was a cruise to the Bahamas. The fest was no disappointment, for we got 100 new members and the opportunity to market to 3000 more potential members. This was one of the best and surely the largest promotion that we had ever had.

The year 1995 was another successful year at Seaboard Credit Union. Our assets were at $71.7 million (wow) and our membership had increased to 13,400. I continued to be in awe of our success and could then understand that when you help people you receive much success!

Summary:

We took a semi-break from marketing to plan for the future. We made plans for our 14,000 square feet signature building. The new building would do marketing for us in the community.

Chapter 17

The business plan for 1996 was very aggressive, and we had a lot of work to do. Remember that I was supposed to be researching the property in the Southpoint business development for purchase to build a new signature home office for Seaboard Credit Union. I could not let this stop us from paying attention to our primary focus helping our members to fulfill their dreams!

The credit union movement always had been a cooperative movement and in Jacksonville, Florida, there was no exception to that mantra. In March 1996, we opened our 4th branch in Orange Park, Florida. This branch was so special because we were sharing it with a much larger and successful credit union than ours, Jax Federal Credit Union. The branch was again state of art with safe deposit boxes, an ATM, and double phone system, one for Seaboard and one for Jax Federal. We continued to still answer our phones with a live person, and therefore, we had to connect our phone system to ours at the main office in the Westside.

This branch emphasized the cooperative spirit of the credit union movement. Not only did we help our members, we helped other credit unions to succeed. A brick and mortar branch was very expensive and what better way for us to afford it than to share it with another credit union. The opening of this branch in Orange Park area opened up a whole realm of membership opportunities. Because the area was a suburb of Jacksonville, we were then moving in another direction; more toward the place where our members lived instead of where they worked. The branch was a huge success of Seaboard and Jax Federal.

We participated in the Juvenile Diabetes Walk in the heat of the summer. We joined our SEG groups and had a huge team. Staff really wanted to participate. We created a shirt with our team logo on it. We received many donations and our team did a fantastic job with this community event. There again we were seen participating with community functions with our SEG groups.

We added a new twist to our fall promotions that continued to bring excitement and free publicity. Our promotions that year were called, "Money Mania", and we rented a money machine, where members could step in a 10- feet box and air blew money around. Whatever you could catch, you could keep. The promotion was a fantastic hit. You had to be a member to participate. We signed up 150 new members at these promotions that year. We had the money mania machine at all promotions in October 1996, including the Halloween promotion in which we were the judges of the costume contest.

The City of Jacksonville had the first Annual Kids Fest that year. We participated and attended the Kid's Fest as a sponsor. We had a booth and saw over 1000 kids at the function. Due to community events like this, we continued to reach our membership goals. We sold our "Dalmation Club" at this event. We signed up more than 35 new children's accounts at this promotion.

By the end of 1996, our assets were just short of $79 million and our membership had increased to over 14,600. What a successful credit union! Wow, 1997 started a very exciting year for Seaboard Credit Union. We had plenty to do. To begin the year, we closed on the purchase of the site in Southpoint where the new signature building would be built. The groundbreaking was held in July 1997, and it was terribly hot! The heat could not dampen our spirits and excitement with the exciting new building plan that began. We had a huge groundbreaking ceremony and many city officials attended. We also had our company picnic on the site in September. All staff and board of directors attended both events. The excitement spread over the entire business complex.

During that year, we had the annual meeting in January. Four-member appreciation events were held in Westside, Southpoint, Orange Park, and Baltimore branches. All the member functions were well attended. Our members loved for us to appreciate them. We opened many new accounts, attained many new members, and our products/service per member ratio remained above national averages.

1997 brought so much growth, fun, and excitement. We far surpassed our growth goals we purchased the site for the new signature building that would propel us into the 21st century and life was great at Seaboard Credit Union. We had almost 16,000 members who had entrusted us with over $86.8 million of their money. We continued to grow and were considered to be in the big league. We were one of the most successful and progressive credit unions in the country. All this success was directly related to our continued service to our members and helping them realize their dreams! Our attitude of gratitude had not diminished over the 18 years of my tenure. Things were really beginning to change in the credit union movement. Federal rules and regulations were putting more emphasis on the net worth of credit unions and less on the growth of credit unions. Many credit unions were outgrowing their net worth. Thanks to our vision at Seaboard Credit Union, we knew and understand that our net worth growth had to beat our asset and membership growth in order for us to sustain and continue to offer the products and services in the manner that our members expected. Over the years, we had set our members' expectations of Seaboard Credit Union at a very high level, which meant that we needed the money in our net worth to sustain it.

In 1998, the atmosphere was changing, credit unions were being merged. They went through a growing downturn in order to meet regulatory requirements of increased capital (net worth) requirements. Seaboard was in a position to avoid having to stunt the asset and membership growth due to the net worth planning over the past 15 years. Therefore, we continued with our five-year plan to have disciplined and steady growth in order to sustain the level of service that our members came to expect.

We began our year-long promotion called, "Moving and Marvelous," in order to prepare our staff and members for the awesome move to the new 14,000 square feet signature building in Southpoint. The year had finally come when we would be moving forward with our plans to propel us into the 21st century. This promotion, "Moving and Marvelous" was a year-long promotion and it took all people involved to plan and implement it. We had many, many functions with staff to prepare them for the growth of the year, the hard work involved with completing the new signature headquarters building as well as the move to the new building, all the while maintaining the level of service that had made us a continued huge success.

"Moving and Marvelous" began with a limousine ride for all staff members to the new site where the building was would be built. This was a wonderful kickoff for the promotion and pumped up staff, inspiring them to work more as most of us had never ridden in a limo. All staff members were given flowers when they arrived at the site. It was a very moving event.

We had the last annual meeting in January at the Westside branch. The following year we would begin to have the annual meetings at the new signature building. This annual meeting was very well attended and all the members and staff were very excited about the steady and planned growth and the strength of Seaboard Credit Union.

Summary:

Plans were moving along nicely. We were growing tremendously. Our marketing and business plans were working because we were working them.

Chapter 18

Success breeds Success! Seaboard Credit Union had another affirmation of the success of the credit union in March 1998. All the progressive credit unions in Jacksonville, Florida were so excited to hear that America Online (AOL) was opening a call center to handle all the calls regarding their services in the Southeast of the country. We all started preparing our proposals to get AOL as a SEG of their credit union. This was the largest group that had come to our city in years. AOL would employ 3,000 in Jacksonville for a total company count of 12,000 and have eight call centers all over the country.

Seaboard took the full service approach on our proposal to add AOL as a company to our SEG groups. Our proposal included dropping ATMs in all eight call centers in order to offer their 12,000 employees the proper service that they deserved. To our astonishment and surprise, AOL accepted our proposal and chose Seaboard Credit Union for their financial institution of choice for their employees and their direct deposits. As of March 1998, Seaboard Credit Union became part of the benefit package of a very large and successful company, America Online (AOL). The fun had begun!

The plan for AOL was a year-long. It would take us a year to implement eight ATMS in their call centers as well as membership promotions in each of their locations. We had three vice presidents that prepared the membership promotions and signed up their employees. Membership drives were held throughout the year at AOL offices. This team of three VPs traveled quite a bit in 1998. This coup for Seaboard created our membership, loan, checking accounts, direct deposits, and transactions numbers for this year. We signed up over 2500 members at AOL, launched five ATMS, and surpassed all goals for the year.

One of the 6 AOL locations and workplace that we had the open enrollment for Seaboard Credit Union

On the home front, we still had a credit union and 16,000 members to service and surpass their expectations. The new signature building was progressing very nicely. We prepared a time capsule to be opened in 25 years that was buried on the front plaza of the new building. This time capsule promotion was very exciting and many members attended the celebration to bury the capsule. Our "Moving and Marvelous" promotion was progressing very nicely. We had many events planned throughout the year to celebrate our success.

In April, we had a staff appreciation steak dinner. The board of directorss were the chefs of this elegant dinner held at our Westside branch. The event was attended by 100% of the invitees. Rewards and recognition were given to our fantastic staff. A happy staff makes happy members. With all the work that we had to do in 1998, this was the least that we could do to continue "Moving and Marvelous"

Grand opening day at the new signature building in Southpoint was held in August 1998. With so many guests, lots of congratulatory flowers, jazz band, 100% staff and Board in attendance, so much glitz and glamour, and so many members in attendance, "Moving and Marvelous" was coming to fruition. The new building was 14,000 square feet of magnificence. Finally, Seaboard Credit Union was ready to go into the 21st century.

The site of the future signature building for us

Sign for new signature building.

The Signature New Building for Seaboard Credit Union – in all her majesty. A little of the old and a little of the new. The new building ran the theme of "Experiencing the Seaboard Touch" and "Moving forward" by portraying these in visual form. The momentum continued to build in 1998.

Seaboard's party that year was more than any of us could wish for. We were recognized by the NFL team, the Jacksonville Jaguars in October 1998. We were honored to have our party at the Jag Fun Zone and attend the game. We were announced on the jumbotron at the game. It was a perfect party full of fun and NFL excitement. Seaboard has become well-known known in the Jacksonville community. We were considered a player.

1998 ended as one of the most exciting years in Seaboard history. I could not have been prouder of our credit union. Our assets were rapidly approaching $100 million and were at $95.8 million and our membership numbers had grown so rapidly to 17,300. We were always sticking to our roots and original mantras of:

"People helping people"
"Making our members' dreams come true"
"High touch/High tech"
"Experience the Seaboard Touch"
"Moving forward and Marvelous"

Summary:
What a year! What successes! The culmination of many years of marketing and helping people. Marketing was the key to our success. Enthusiasm and passion galore for success.

Chapter 19

1999 brought us to preparing for Y2K (year 2000). The annual meeting in 1999 was a tremendous success. It was held at the new signature building in Southpoint and many, many members attended. We had a lot of successes to share from the previous 20 years of my tenure. The annual meeting was a combination of financial reports for 1998 and my 20 years of service. I was given a trophy for my 20 years of service. It was a huge crystal diamond with the inscription reading, "Nancy Mattox – Seaboard's Jewel." There were lots of fun, congratulations, and tears at this well attended annual meeting.

Y2K was a phenomena that was way overrated. Because we had upgraded our legacy data processing system, we had not expected issues with Y2K. Due to regulatory concerns, all credit unions were required to have a Y2K plan. This plan took many man hours to prepare and test for Y2K. We were prepared for the technology clocks to turn on January 1, 2000. We properly tested and retested our systems to ensure no issues.

The plan for the membership drives at the AOL locations were continued to be implemented that year. We had a huge promotion at the AOL call center in Jacksonville. The place was very much high tech, and we learned a lot from the employees at the call center. We also had a huge promotion at the AOL call center in Utah. The ATMS were deployed to the AOL locations. The plan was almost completed without any issues.

In July, we had a member appreciation promotion at our new signature building. We served hot dogs, sodas, and chips. Members came from all around to enjoy the promotion. We were still running our $5 for new members' promotion and we really played this up at this community event. We opened 30 new accounts. A huge success!

In August, we had a new car sale on our lot in Southpoint. Enterprise Car Sales was very popular at this time. Most credit unions had sales. Ours was a little different and a first for Jacksonville area credit unions. Our lot was large enough to accommodate the sale. Enterprise brought more than 100 units and set them up on our site. Other credit unions participated in the Enterprise Car Sale. There were tents, cars, balloons, radio broadcasting, and many members in attendance. We gleaned 25 car loans from the sale. It was very successful!

In October, we had a member appreciation promotion at our Westside branch. This promotion was special because we had the Jacksonville Jaguars mascot, Jackson D Ville in attendance. We had games set up and plenty of fun. Jackson made the promotion a huge success, and we increased our product/service per member ratio again.

We had our Halloween promotion at the CSX Southpoint building, with tents, food, and judges for the costume contest. This event had grown to more than 1000 in attendance from year to year. It allowed us much needed access to our members, potential members, and the buildings in Southpoint. We were on a first name basis with employees, which let us in when we needed to promote and deliver. By the end of 1999, we had reached another milestone at Seaboard Credit Union.

Our assets grew to $105 million (bigger league) and our members were at 17,300. Wow, what a year! These were more blessings to Seaboard Credit Union because we were blessing over 17,300 members with great service and products, making their dreams come true. Our focus was still, "People helping people."

Summary:
Key to success. Another milestone of $105 million in assets with over 17,000 members. Our marketing has worked, hard work has produced results, great and happy staff helped, and living proof that passion for people and helping people work.

Chapter 20

Year 2000 had finally arrived. It seemed impossible that I had been at the credit union for 22 years and that we were serving more than 17,000 members and allowed to manage $105 million of their hard-earned money. But it was true. Year 2000 would prove to be another banner year for Seaboard Credit Union.

We began in January 2000 with our annual meeting. The annual meeting was held at our signature building in Southpoint. Members were so excited to come to the building and the annual meeting. We had so much success to share! We all reminisced about the size of the credit union, how many people we were serving, and how we had a strong financially healthy financial institution. Our railroaders were so happy to have begun the credit union and for its continuation.

In March, we had a huge celebration and staff appreciation event. One of our VPs had been with us for 20 years and had given much of her life to the success of Seaboard Credit Union. The event was fantastic, fun filled, and made the staff ready to move forward and help our members and grow the credit union. Happy employees made for happy members, which made for a successful credit union.

Our major promotion in 2000 was "Money Mania." We rented the money machine and took it with us to over 10 locations. The membership promotion was a huge success bringing in more than 350 members. This money machine, which we had used before, allowed the members to get in the box with money flying all around. The more money they could catch, the more money they could keep. The rewards, publicity, and free advertisement from this promotion in which we got 350 new members, far outweighed the cost of the promotion.This promotion was another Seaboard success and great example of guerilla marketing. We went to our members and potential members!

We were approached by the Jacksonville Sheriff's Office in July 2000. They wanted to propose to buy our Westside building. We had downsized the branch when we opened the new signature building in Southpoint. The Sheriff wanted to open a police substation in the front part of the building. This part of the building was not where the safe deposit boxes and drives-thru were. We decided to sell the building to the JSO, and the work began to convert the front half of the building to be the substation and the rear of the building would still be Seaboard Credit Union's Westside branch. This was a winning combination for the neighborhood, surrounding businesses, the credit union, and the sheriff's office. All city dignitaries were at the Grand Opening of the JSO substation. Another coup for Seaboard Credit Union was to be a fan of the community. We received a lot of free positive publicity.

The Halloween and Costume Contest promotion at Southpoint had grown so much that we were still involved; we had an outdoor tent, served hotdogs and sodas, judged the contest, and got more goodwill from CSX than anyone could imagine.

Year 2000 was a great year for Seaboard Credit Union. We grew our membership to 20,600 members with $115.5 in assets. Another five-year plan was successfully completed and the next five-year plan held as much excitement and growth.

Summary:

Now we are realizing the exponential growth because of our constant "stay on target" marketing. Our perseverance has worked. Our hard work and endless hours of marketing have worked.

Chapter 21

The next three years were so special to me. I was preparing for retirement in 2003, when I had 25 years of service. I wanted 2001, 2002, and 2003 to be our finest years since I would be retiring in 2003. Our members did not fail me. We worked our five-year plan and continued to prosper and grow soundly using the guerilla marketing plan.

We continued to have our member appreciations at our off site locations, we continued to have our Christmas parties for staff, we continued to have our staff recognitions, and we continued our fabulous promotions throughout the years of 2001, 2002, and 2003. We surpassed our goals and worked our five-year business plan. We were still humbled by the success of the credit union and the amount of goodwill that we were able to offer.

In 2001, our assets were $127 million and we had more than 22,500 members.

In 2002, our assets were $138 million and we had more than 24,000 members.

As my tenure rapidly approached the end, after 25 years of being CEO/President, and after 25 years of serving our
members and turning 50 in April 2003, my run was over. I would not have missed that dance for the world.

In 2003, Seaboard Credit Union was a highly successful credit union with $150.3 million in assets and serviced 25,300 members.

I couldn't have been happier and more pleased that I was able to serve our members, grow our credit union in a stable and safe manner, and retire on a high note.

Summary:

What a wonderful and fantastic ride of my life. I made it all that it can be. Utilized my God given talent to help people and never lose sight of that talent. My passion, compassion, and can do attitude brought me many many years of joy and success.

Chapter 22

How to grow and develop any small business:

It is relative easy to grow your small business. You must decide how much you want to grow and how to accomplish the growth. You must be totally committed to 100% to grow your business. You must be all IN! It is all about bringing your products and services to your customers (members). What you think about your bring about!

You must first begin with marketing goals. Keep these goals to a minimum of 4 goals. Make the goals balanced and obtainable. Break them down to the lowest number by daily or monthly. Daily and monthly goals are easier to monitor as well as staff can take the medicine in smaller doses.

Sample Marketing Plan:

June 2014	July 2014	August 2014
6-26 – 6-30 trip to Credit Union for onsite Promotion for new members & loans 50 new members 15 new loans Present marketing plan and goals for 2014/2015	*7-8 – 7-9 trip to Credit Union for onsite Promotion for new members & loans 50 new members 15 new loans Attend any Community functions and set up a table Promote Car Loans (already financed) and Fresh Start loans Increase CL/CD sales Promote Checking accounts with DD Weekly – set up tables at major sponsors and all affiliates Flyers on cars in parking lots	*8-15 – 8-17 trip to Credit Union for onsite promotions 50 new members 50 new loans Attend any Community functions and set up a table Promote Car Loans (already financed) and Fresh Start loans Increase CL/CD sales Promote Checking accounts with DD Community awareness – Credit 101 seminar Weekly – set up tables at sponsors and all affiliates Flyers on cars in parking lots Door Hangers in nearby neighborhoods and apartment complexes

Nancy Gail Smith Mattox

December 2014	January 2015	February 2015

Onsite promotions
  50 new members
  100 new loans
Attend any CSRA functions and set up a table
Promote Car Loans (already financed) and Fresh Start loans
Increase CL/CD sales
Increase IDT sales
Roll out GI Life insurance
Promote Checking accounts with DD
Community awareness – Credit 101 seminar
Weekly – set up tables at Sponsors and all affiliates
Flyers on cars in parking lots
Door Hangers in nearby neighborhoods and apartment complexes
	Onsite promotions
	  50 new members
	  100 new loans
	Attend any CSRA functions and set up a table
	Promote Car Loans (already financed) and Fresh Start loans
	Increase CL/CD sales
	Increase IDT sales
	Increase GI Life insurance sales
	Promote Checking accounts with DD
	Community awareness – Credit 101 seminar
	Weekly – set up tables at Sponsors and all affiliates
	Flyers on cars in parking lots
	Door Hangers in nearby neighborhoods and apartment complexes
		Onsite promotions
		  50 new members
		  100 new loans
		Attend any CSRA functions and set up a table
		Promote Car Loans (already financed) and Fresh Start loans
		Increase CL/CD sales
		Increase IDT sales
		Increase GI Life insurance sales
		Promote Checking accounts with DD
		Community awareness – Credit 101 seminar
		Weekly – set up tables at Sponsors and all affiliates
		Flyers on cars in parking lots
		Door Hangers in nearby neighborhoods and apartment complexes

March 2015	April 2015	May 2015

Onsite promotions
  50 new members
  100 new loans
Attend any CSRA functions and set up a table
Promote Car Loans (already financed) and Fresh Start loans
Increase CL/CD sales
Increase IDT sales
Increase GI Life insurance sales
Promote Checking accounts with DD
UNFCU community awareness – Credit 101 seminar
Weekly – set up tables at sponsors and all affiliates
Flyers on cars in parking lots
Door Hangers in nearby neighborhoods and apartment complexes
	Onsite promotions
	  50 new members
	  100 new loans
	Attend any CSRA functions and set up a table
	Promote Car Loans (already financed) and Fresh Start loans
	Increase CL/CD sales
	Increase IDT sales
	Increase GI Life insurance sales
	Promote Checking accounts with DD
	UNFCU community awareness – Credit 101 seminar
	Weekly – set up tables at sponsors and all affiliates
	Flyers on cars in parking lots
	Door Hangers in nearby neighborhoods and apartment complexes
		Onsite promotions
		  50 new members
		  100 new loans
		Attend any CSRA functions and set up a table
		Promote Car Loans (already financed) and Fresh Start loans
		Increase CL/CD sales
		Increase IDT sales
		Increase GI Life insurance sales
		Promote Checking accounts with DD
		UNFCU community awareness – Credit 101 seminar
		Weekly – set up tables at sponsors and all affiliates
		Flyers on cars in parking lots
		Door Hangers in nearby neighborhoods and apartment complexes

Nancy Gail Smith Mattox

Chapter 23

Keys to Success:

- Hard work seeking tangible and proven results through the Marketing, Growth and Expansion Plan using a milestone strategy. Marketing, Growth, and Expansion goals must be obtainable. They need to be monitored constantly bringing it down to the lowest level (i.e. daily or monthly). Hard working staff members will be able to absorb the expansion concepts because monthly reports will be kept on a daily basis. Comparisons to previous months, previous months last year are very important for monitoring. Staff must understand what all the hard work will bring. Monitoring will bring about the milestone strategy. Every milestone met will need excitement and enthusiasm to keep all motivated.

- Promote products and services 100% of the time. Knowledge of products and services is paramount for the success of the expansion plans. Anywhere that your customers meet, you must meet and have a promotion table to talk about what you do and how you do it. Growing your business is an obsession that you must have. Always have your business cards and marketing brochures with you. There is a 5 feet rule, which is anyone that comes within 5 feet of you no matter where you are (grocery store, barber shop, shopping mall, restaurants, pharmacist, picking up kids school, utilities, vacation, camping), should be marketed to about your business. Your business is your business. You live, eat, drink your business 100% of the time. You will wake up one day and the magic will have happened. You will have more customers that you thought possible.

- Strive to offer the BEST service. Hire only marketing and customer service people. Happy staff make happy customers! Period, no excuses. If you determine that you have made a hiring mistake, end it immediately......You must train your staff to help customers. Staff must be able to have a "people helping people" attitude. Their one goal in life while working for you should be to help the customers. They must get on the level and speak to them about helping them. There should never be any degrading of any customer. Their thoughts of the customers should not be relayed to the customer or co-workers. If you can't say something good, then say nothing at all. Staff must always fight for the customer, whatever it takes to help them. Always be sincere and help people and you will have loyal customers for life. You and your company will prosper way beyond your dreams if you following this one concept.

- Our Products and Services are the BEST. You and the staff MUST believe this with all their being. No other company can hold a candle to our products and services. They are the best, period. Whatever it takes to keep these products and services the best must be done. If it means, bundling products to get the sale, so be it. Maybe one product or service standing alone may not be the best, but the combination of several plus the excellent staff will make it the best. Staff must be able to close the sale and make the customer happy. Customers must be happy enough to recommend the company to their circle of influence. It can happen. It is magic how growth will happen. Your phones will be blowing up to get the great service and the best products.

- Maintain profitability at levels to meet or succeed growth goals (i.e. balanced growth). Profit is king! Every penny spent on the marketing, growth, and expansion MUST bring enough in for the company to be profitable. As the owner, you must make sure that you have balanced growth. The pricing of the products and services to sell, must have profitability built in and still let it be competitive. Mind your business!

- Market where potential customers meet. Potential customers can be anywhere that you are. Remember the 5 feet rule! Anyone that comes with 5 feet of you should be your target. If you children play sports, then you have 100's of potential customers. If you go to church, you have 100's of potential customers. If your children take dance lessons or gymnastics, you have 100's of potential customers. All of your friends and family members are your warm market. Turn every event into a marketing opportunity. Never stop talking about your products and services. You can't be shy. You must be proud of your business. If you must set up a table and offer snacks (popcorn does very well) do it. People love to talk and visit, always turn this into an opportunity for your business.

- Attend community events (i.e. festivals, fairs, chamber of commerce, lions clubs, parades, etc.). You should be a member of all clubs in your area. Exposure is the key to expansion. You must expose your business at every event that you can. If you have 3 or 4 employees, send 1 to each event. Set up a table, always speak, always have a giveaway (door prize). Get leads by having people register for the door prize. It is very important to get the name, phone number, and email address. Always, always follow up on leads that you get. If they apply for your door prize, you have already talked to them, so they are not strangers any longer. This makes the call a warm call not a cold call. You could also co-op with other companies to share in expenses for the events (table costs, door prize, and snacks).

- Market on social media. An absolute MUST!!!!! No exceptions. Most companies already have the social media in place. Assign someone in the office to maintain and post to the social media several times a day. Remember exposure is everything in expanding your business. Post anything to get your business' name out on social media. Have contests on social media. People need light hearted information in our most complicated world. Be on Facebook, twitter, linked in, and all other social medias. This does not take a whole lot of time, just a few minutes a few times a day. We love to business from social media, as we can repost and get more customers.

- We will grow into a viable and competitive small business. Set your goals and monitor the progress. You should see results in 90 days if you are following all the suggestions. After a year, you will have to adjust your goals and increase them. You will have the income to do so. Your business must be important to your customers. Service is the key. Loyalty will be created by great customer service. Loyal customers that have been treated well will not even consider looking much less moving to another business for their products and services.

- We will know our customers. This is key to maintain your loyal customer base. When you see them, you know them, you know how to converse with them and you do not ever let an opportunity slip through the cracks. Never, never be too busy to speak to your customers and find out what is happening in their lives. You never know when something has changed and they may need to use more of your products and services.

- We will change the lives of our customers by offering stellar products and services. Relationships are important. In order to change a person's life, we must be able to know how they feel and what is happening. We must have the types of relationship with our customers so that we know which of products and services are right for them at the right time.

Expansion and continuity of your business depends on it. Make it happen. No excuses!

- We will offer our members dreams! Do everything in your power to learn what makes your customers tick. You must know what they dream about. You must maneuver to fulfil their dreams whatever they may be. Work the dreams of your customers into your business plans, marketing plans, products and services and you will have an unbelievable amount of loyalty and referrals from your existing customers. More success!

- What we think about we bring about! A positive mental attitude regarding our businesses and lives is KEY! I remember always teaching my golfing son about a PMA (positive mental attitude). It was his mantra. He even wrote PMA on his golf hats and golf balls while in college playing in tournaments. He learned to leave the last shot and move onto the next shot with a positive mental attitude. Therefore, he had to think about his next shot so that he could bring it about! The same concept works for businesses. Always have a PMA. Make it part of your being. Make it part of your expansion plans. You will experience success way beyond your wildest dreams. I did this with my career and helped thousands of people to have a PMA. I fulfilled their dreams. It was not an option for me not to. What we think about we bring about! Proven 100's of times in my life and my son's life.

Chapter 24

Words of Wisdom

Process for procuring an appointment and making a presentation. Yes, cold calling!

- Be persistent. It takes at least 7 phone calls to get past the gatekeeper in order to even set the appointment.
- Always be sincere. Do not be condescending.
- Give the prospect the respect that they deserve for their position
- Always know your prospect. Review everything you can about them. Use social media, google, and know them inside and out before talking to them.
- Always be ten minutes early. Never, never be late or postpone. Do not call to verify appointment. This gives them the chance to back out.
- Always be professional. Look the part of your company. We have standard uniforms to wear when we are working for the company.
- Get to the point quickly. Be pleasant, then talk about your product. Take notes during the question and answer period. Don't interrupt.
- Separate yourself from the competition. For example, my company has a unique opportunity for publishing books. We distribute on the international market place and prepare a media kit for marketing the new author to the next level, which includes more book sales and motivational speaking engagements. I emphasize our difference.
- Use humor and manners when speaking your presentation. Always talk about them. Mention their pictures in their office. Be confident, not cocky. Build rapport with the client. Act as if the deal is done.

- Play on their interests. In my case, I am always talking to pastors and religious leaders. I am genuinely interested in their life and ministry.
- Always be positive, enthusiastic, focused, polished, honest and convinced.
- Always be outstanding so that they remember you and your company
- Follow up with a handwritten note thank them for their time.
- Try to be a familiar face in the audiences where they are speaking or meeting.
- Always meet and greet them as if you have known them forever.
- Be genuine.
- Stay in their mind and on their mid.

Pitfalls
- Be careful and do not mix up the accomplishments of the client with other clients.
- Always know your presentation
- Be prepared to respond honestly to all questions, if you don't know the answer, politely say that you will have to check on that.
- Don't name drop.
- Make them your world and center of attention
- Always call them by their name with title: (i.e. Bishop Smith, Pastor Davis, Reverend Jones, etc.)
- Everyone loves to hear their own name
- Do NOT oversell yourself or product
- Make sure that your company can deliver on what you have told the client (i.e. deadlines, targets, and milestones)
- Be careful of being trapped into speaking of others in the same field.
- Do not be pushy or try to rush your client.

- Be trustworthy
- Be available for questions
- Always return phone calls and or message as soon as possible - this makes you and your company reliable
- Do not assume

www.ingramcontent.com/pod-product-compliance
Lightning Source LLC
Chambersburg PA
CBHW021440170526
45164CB00001B/323